How to Form Networks for School Renewal

Lew Allen and Barbara Lunsford

How to
Form
Networks
for School
Renewal

Lew Allen and Barbara Lunsford

Association for Supervision and Curriculum Development
Alexandria, Virginia

About the Authors
Lew Allen is Director of Outreach, Program for School Improvement, and Barbara Lunsford is Director of the League of Professional Schools, College of Education, University of Georgia. Both can be reached at the University of Georgia, 124 Aderhold Hall, Athens, GA 30602; telephone: (706) 542-2516.

Association for Supervision and Curriculum Development
1250 N. Pitt Street, Alexandria, VA 22314
Telephone: (703) 549-9110 FAX: (703) 549-3891

Printed in the United States of America.

Ronald S. Brandt, *Executive Editor*
Nancy Carter Modrak, *Managing Editor, ASCD Books*
Margaret A. Oosterman, *Associate Editor*
Gary Bloom, *Manager, Design and Production Services*
Stephanie Justen, *Production Coordinator*
Valerie Sprague, *Desktop Publisher*

From the Editors:
We welcome readers' comments on ASCD books and other publications. If you would like to give us your opinion of this book or suggest topics for future books, please write to ASCD, Managing Editor of Books, 1250 N. Pitt St., Alexandria, VA 22314.

ASCD Stock Number: 1-95038; price: $6.95

Library of Congress Cataloging-in-Publication Data

Allen, Lew, 1947-
    How to form networks for school renewal / Lew Allen and Barbara Lunsford.
      p.   cm.
    "ASCD stock number: 1-95038"—T.p. verso.
    Includes bibliographical references.
    ISBN 0-87120-242-5 : $6.95
    1. Teachers—Social networks—United States. 2. Educational change—United States. I. Lunsford, Barbara. II. Association for Supervision and Curriculum Development. III. Title.
LB1775.2.A44 1995
371.1—dc20   95-5355
                                                     CIP

How to Form Networks for School Renewal

Foreword

I RECENTLY ATTENDED A MEETING OF MAJOR SCHOOL RENEWAL networks in the United States. Teachers and principals from our network, the League of Professional Schools, met with similar representatives from other national networks: Coalition of Essential Schools; Comer Schools; Accelerated Schools Project; Success for All; and Foxfire Fund. This networking of the networks was one of the first times that educators from a number of national networks had an opportunity to share candidly with each other the nature of their work, their successes, failures, and future plans. We realized we have much in common:

• Our networks are not projects set for a finite period of time.

• We are a way of connecting schools to conduct ongoing, "generational" work on purposeful and positive educational change.

• We are guided by principles and premises of educational change—not by prescriptions or packets for schools to follow.

• Our networks exist because of the voluntary will of schools wishing to participate.

• We believe that true reform must come from local sources, with coordination and assistance from school districts, state departments, regional agencies, universities, and other organizations. Our goal is to build a critical mass of schools and personnel who can "do" the hard work of educational change to demonstrate that such positive change can occur in virtually every school and district in the United States.

• We are trying to figure out how to build practitioner faculties from our existing schools to work as facilitators at other schools—without distracting practitioners from efforts in their own schools.

• We all have waiting lists of schools wishing to participate.

This networking of the networks was a valuable learning experience and one we plan to continue. *How to Form Networks for School Renewal* comes at an opportune time—interest in school renewal networks is growing. The League of Professional Schools has received many calls from schools, districts, universities, and state agencies asking how to either join our League or form their own network of schools. Dr. Lew Allen, a former high school teacher, and Dr. Barbara Lunsford, a former school principal, have been key people in consulting, advising, and hosting organizations from across the United States and provinces in North America, Australia, New Zealand, and Korea. These organizations are interested in how the League started; developed additional networks; provided support; and continued to stay true to democratically derived, ongoing, and purposeful educational change.

The authors have written a readable and practical book. It contains examples, protocols, and guides on how the League works. They know what they are talking about. They have spent much time in the field researching and documenting the lessons that are shared here.

In the long run, what particular renewal network a school belongs to or whether the network is coordinated by a district, state, university, or schools themselves is not important. What is important is acknowledging that site-based educational change is tough, ongoing professional work loaded with complexities. Every willing school in the United States deserves to have the chance and the support to work with other schools striving to provide a good education for all students. Such a challenge demands the proliferation of networks to provide access to these schools. This book brings that dream closer to reality.

CARL GLICKMAN
Chair, Program for School Improvement
Professor of Education
University of Georgia

Acknowledgments

THIS BOOK WAS POSSIBLE BECAUSE OF THE EXPERTISE OF THE practitioners with whom we work every day. They taught us the lessons that are included here. We would like to thank Karen Allen, Melba Deen, Robert Bussey, Tom Morris, and Nancy Amulera Marshall for serving as chairs of the League's Congress. We acknowledge Emily Calhoun, the League's first director, for her work in getting this successful and exciting venture off and running and for her continued support as a League associate. Thanks to the following organizations for their support: the BellSouth Foundation; the U.S. Department of Education's National Diffusion Network; the Lettie Pate Evans Foundation, Inc.; the Pittulloch Foundation; the University of Georgia's College of Education; and the Georgia State Department of Education. Finally, we would like to thank Carl Glickman, the founder and chair of the League of Professional Schools. Carl's leadership has been the key element in the learning process that has brought us to this point. His respect and faith in school-based educators, his uncanny ability to not only keep the big picture in mind but to communicate it to others, and his scholarship have put in motion a significant educational movement.

Introduction

HOW TO FORM NETWORKS FOR SCHOOL RENEWAL OFFERS PRACTICAL
guidelines and suggestions on how to establish, maintain,
and evaluate a unique type of network, one that is
practitioner driven. *Practitioner driven* means that
practitioners create and govern the networks, which are
focused on them. Such networks provide school-based
educators with an environment of their own making and
under their control—it focuses on schoolwide concerns.
These networks provide ongoing and frequent
opportunities for people from one school to form collegial
partnerships with people in other schools. They can lean
on, learn from, and inspire each other in renewing their
school's efforts.

This book is written for educators (i.e., teachers,
principals, central office administrators, university faculty,
and area educational agency staff) who are interested in
exploring a new way to facilitate schools' efforts to serve
students better. The information and examples we share are
based on our work with schools who are members of the
League of Professional Schools, a practitioner-driven
network that is making a difference in the lives of teachers,
administrators, and students.

Since its formation in 1989, the League has expanded to
two networks of Georgia schools, one statewide and one
urban. A third network is in development. Membership has
grown to include about 90 elementary, middle, and
secondary schools in rural, urban, and suburban areas.
These schools focus on improving instruction by
implementing shared decision making and conducting
action research.

The League is a university-school partnership; its
partner is the Program for School Improvement (PSI) of the
University of Georgia's college of education. PSI is the

network facilitator, working with the member schools to help carry out the network's premises.

Practitioner-driven networks can also be facilitated by such groups as area education agencies, school districts, state departments, and individual educators hired specifically for the job. In fact, we are currently working with three new networks, none of which will be facilitated by a university.

The League's work has been featured in the *Journal of Staff Development, Educational Leadership, NASSP Bulletin, The Video Journal of Education,* and *Reshaping the Principalship: Insights from Transformational Reform Efforts.* The League is a member of the National Center for Restructuring Education, Schools, and Teaching (NCREST) at Teachers College, Columbia University. The center is a national network of organizations working with renewing schools.

In 1991, 1992, and 1993, PSI and the League received the Anderson Certificate of Merit, an award given to top educational collaborations in the United States. The League's effectiveness in helping schools renew their efforts has been validated by the National Diffusion Network of the U.S. Department of Education.

A belief in democratic decision-making processes, as opposed to hierarchical, bureaucratic processes, drives the League's work. Although networks may be formed without this particular foundation, we write as though it is a given. The reasons become apparent as we describe the purposes and functions of practitioner-driven networks. (See Glickman 1993 for a detailed discussion on democracy's role in school renewal.)

The first chapter focuses on why practitioner-driven networks can be helpful to schools engaged in renewal efforts. We hope that readers will see enough promise in this type of networking to want to know more. In Chapter 2, we discuss what decisions need to be made in getting started, why a clear focus is important, and how to establish a democratic governance process. Chapter 3 explores operational procedures and services that a network might offer member schools to facilitate their efforts. Chapter 4 addresses ongoing issues that a network must face to maintain its effectiveness. Chapter 5 provides an example of how practitioners can be involved in the life of a network by describing the League's Action Research Consortium. Chapter 6 explains activities that can help a network evaluate its effects on member schools.

Please note that we use the terms *school-based educators, teachers and principals,* and *practitioners* to describe our targeted audience for practitioner-driven networks. These terms include *teachers, principals, assistant principals, counselors, social workers, paraprofessionals, parent volunteers, secretaries,* and *cafeteria workers*—anyone whose work is based in schools.

Throughout the book, we use examples from the League's work to show how thoughts can be translated into actions. An icon of a schoolhouse introduces each example:

1
Why Network?

- "I'm seeing more excitement about learning, more ownership of what's going on in this school than I ever have before."
- "It isn't perfect, but it's better than anything out there. We've made tremendous progress. Still have a long way to go."
- "We've come a long way. People like attending League meetings. They come back excited. They are learning and finding contacts with other schools. Teachers are participating in our initiatives, and that tells me we are on the right track. We don't feel like we have arrived but [we] keep trying and working hard. We don't want to go back."

These comments from educators refer to their school's involvement with the League of Professional Schools. The League is an example of what we call a practitioner-driven network. *Practitioner-driven* reflects the idea that such networks are not organizations that schools simply join and then passively follow existing operating procedures. In practitioner-driven networks, the practitioners decide what services they want. They constantly monitor network activities, modify them to meet changing needs, and play key roles in the network leadership. As a practitioner-driven network, the League assists its member schools in many areas:

- Provides regularly scheduled meetings where school teams can share their work.
- Encourages across-school collaborations by involving teachers and principals in visiting other member schools.
- Urges and supports school-based people to share their expertise by publishing network newsletters and monographs that feature their writing.

• Involves educators in the network through the League Congress, ongoing consortiums, and ad hoc task forces.

Teachers and principals report that participating in this network has been a growth-producing, rejuvenating experience that is unique professionally.

Being an effective teacher or principal is challenging work that requires support, enrichment, and encouragement. We have found that one of the best ways for these educators to get this type of help is through networking with other teachers and principals. This may sound like a basic activity, yet it rarely happens. Typically, schools or school systems seeking help and guidance look outside rather than inside schools. Why? Part of the answer may be as simple as availability.

A number of professionals based outside schools are available to help school-based educators. For example, central office staff, university faculty, private consultants, professional organization staff, and school supply and textbook company representatives generally have clearly defined roles and structures that assist them in providing help. Central office staff use policies, guidelines, and job descriptions to organize and focus their helping efforts; university faculty offer courses and workshops. But the group of educators with the most intimate knowledge of what teachers and principals face each day is other teachers and principals—and they are typically not available. They do not have a forum to offer their help.

School-based educators can also be described as school-bound educators because they rarely venture outside their classrooms or schools to share what they have learned with other school-based educators. A typical inservice day for most teachers finds them in their classrooms working by themselves, in the media center or auditorium with their colleagues listening to a prominent expert, or at a central location with teachers from the district listening to an even more prominent expert. Teachers and principals are rarely given opportunities to turn to other teachers and principals, either from within their schools or from other schools, to share *their* expertise.

This lack of opportunity is a critical oversight that practitioner-driven networks can address. We have found that when school-based educators are given ongoing opportunities to network across schools, their professional knowledge, motivation, self-esteem, and, ultimately, their effectiveness in renewing their efforts with students increase dramatically.

We are not suggesting that networks should replace other ways of helping schools. Educators need many different sources of help. And we certainly aren't suggesting doing away with central office personnel. Their role is critical. We are suggesting establishing a balance. For too long, schools and school districts have only looked to those based outside schools as possible resources and ignored the wealth of expertise found in schools.

A six-member team from each of the League's member schools attends a two-day conference. On the first morning, participants hear a keynote address by a noted educator. She delivers a lively, fast-paced talk on assessment, a topic of great interest. She is given a standing ovation. After the address, she is swamped by people who want more information or simply to meet her.

The remaining conference time provides opportunities for participants to meet with the speaker and university faculty in more informal settings, where they can make points of their own or ask questions of specific interest to them. Breakout sessions are also part of the agenda. University-based educators conduct some sessions; teachers, principals, guidance counselors, paraprofessionals, and parents who are implementing the featured innovations direct most of them.

Conference evaluations reveal what was expected— participants loved the keynote address. They were carried away by the speaker's charismatic way of presenting new, exciting information in such a dramatic fashion. When the participants were asked which part of the conference was of most value to them, however, the most frequent response was "hearing from other school people." They found hearing about what others were doing in their schools, both in formal presentations and in informal settings such as the hallways, was the type of information that was most likely to be incorporated into their work when they went home. They didn't say they didn't want to hear from educators based outside schools. They do. But the most frequent suggestion on what should be considered in planning the next year's conference was "provide more time for us to spend with other school people." This scenario has been repeated over and over during the five years of the League's existence. What is going on here? What do teachers and principals get from spending time with other teachers and principals?

Credibility

Teachers value opportunities to learn from other teachers more than from any other source (Smylie 1994). When teachers and principals interact with other teachers and principals, they get credible ideas that spark their thinking and inform their practice. School-based educators confer a high level of credibility to the ideas and suggestions of their peers. They may not give that same level to the ideas of those based outside schools. When a teacher hears an idea from another teacher, the when-was-the-last-time-you-were-in-the-classroom syndrome doesn't occur. A teacher talks about her experiences at League meetings: "Every time you come here . . . you learn so much because these are teachers talking. Teachers saying what they do and they tell us what works and what doesn't work."

Affirmation

A typical comment heard at League meetings is "We thought we were the only ones struggling with this problem. We feel much better about ourselves and our work knowing other schools are having some of the same problems we are." When a school works in isolation, staff have no way of knowing if their struggles are normal or if something is wrong with them. Networking helps them affirm what they are doing, puts their work in perspective with others who are doing similar work in similar situations, and encourages them to keep working, knowing that others are experiencing the same difficulties.

In reporting on a case study about a school's involvement in a multischool project, Short and Greer (1993) noted a similar finding:

Four staff members went to visit another project school in
another state. It was important to the faculty at Crestview
to discover that the process of change in their school was
similar to the challenges being experienced elsewhere.
The teachers had an opportunity to discuss and exchange
ideas with the faculty at the other school. These
discussions reinforced a sense of collaboration (p. 179).

Energy

Teachers and principals find sharing and listening to
other teachers and principals energizing. For example,
when Jane is asked to make a presentation about something
her school is doing, several positive things happen. First,
she feels good that her peers think enough about what she
and her colleagues are doing to ask her to share. She feels
valued and professional. Second, making a presentation
about her work is revitalizing and motivational. As she
reflects on what elements of her work are worth sharing,
she feels a sense of professional pride and is perhaps
pleased at the progress that has been made. While making
the presentation, she finds having a group of peers who
listen and ask questions about what she is doing to be a
heady experience. After the presentation, members of the
audience return to their schools with ideas they know they
can actually use in classrooms. Jane returns to her school
rejuvenated, validated professionally, and ready to continue
the exhausting work of being an effective teacher.

A teacher speaks about her experiences in the League:
"Through the League, I have been asked to speak at several
different conferences. I've spoken at several different
schools, and as a teacher I have grown professionally. . . .
It's changed my whole attitude as a professional."

Reflection

To share what you are doing, you must first reflect
inwardly and then with colleagues about what needs to be
covered in a presentation. What are the key elements of
what we are doing? Why are we doing this and not that?
This reflection may bring new insights.

After studying a school district that provided opportunities for across-school communication, Firestone and Bader (1992) concluded, "the expectation that . . . teachers [will] interact with their colleagues encouraged all involved to think through student needs more carefully. There was also greater reflection on instructional practice" (p. 207). Practitioner-driven networks provide ongoing opportunities for such reflection.

Nonpolitical Environment

Teachers and principals find that working across schools with colleagues who have a firsthand understanding of their problems and working conditions creates a secure, nonpolitical environment that encourages sharing concerns and seeking help. Professionals do not feel the need to put a positive spin on everything that they're doing or to hide or downplay difficulties they're experiencing. Practitioner-driven networks can create an atmosphere without evaluations or competition for hierarchical positions. They can be safe havens where, as Lieberman and McLaughlin (1992) state, people can "act as both experts and apprentices, teachers and learners" (p. 674).

Key Points

- Practitioner-driven networks can provide school-based educators with ongoing professional development opportunities not found in individual schools, school districts, university programs, or professional organizations.
- A network should not be seen as a laboratory where practitioners do the work and the network facilitator monitors and evaluates practitioners' efforts. The climate surrounding a network should be collegial and free of hierarchical structures.
- The push should constantly be toward practitioners taking an active role in network activities. Practitioners should both receive and provide services.

2
Beginnings

As a shampoo commercial points out, "You only have one chance to make a first impression." The initial contacts between a possible facilitator and school-based educators are crucial when putting a network together. Key decisions must be made and patterns of operation established.

Initial Contact with Schools

Conversation about a school's associating with a network should begin in the school: A school should not be forced or pressured to join a network. Of course, a school may involve people from outside, but teachers and principals should discuss their school's possible membership without anyone in a hierarchical position unduly influencing them. As the educators closest to where instructional and curricular decisions get played out, school-based people should be the decision-making unit and occupy key roles in a network's governance and activities. After a school decides to join a network, the district can play a central role in helping the school take full advantage of its network membership.

Initial contacts with schools should involve school teams rather than individuals (e.g., principal, lead teacher, or other school representative). Networks that stress teamwork and involving many people from the beginning can better help schools build common visions about what the schools want to accomplish. Such networks can also help develop schoolwide perspectives on issues. Involving several educators from a school in the initial conversation can also help limit the perception that this thing being considered is someone's pet project.

The principal should play a part in a school's deliberations. This participation may seem obvious, but we have had held workshops for school teams to consider joining the League and the principal did not attend—sometimes in an effort to not be seen as trying to push the school's membership and sometimes out of indifference. In most school systems, the decision-making authority lies with the principal, who is directly responsible for what goes on in the school building. Because a practitioner-driven network requires that schools spend resources to be active members, the principal must be part of the initial conversation.

Defining Network Focus

Before commitments are made to form a practitioner-driven network, both the facilitator and the schools considering membership should have a clear understanding of what the network's focus will be. An organization that already has a focus or a group of schools that has a shared set of priorities can start a network. Those involved must be clear about the network's purpose and the common beliefs, practices, and approaches that will hold the schools together despite their individual differences. Belonging to a network means having an identity, or a mission, that distinguishes members from other schools. A school's membership should indicate what the educators in that school believe and strive to achieve.

The League of Professional Schools was started when the Program for School Improvement sent a letter to all public schools in Georgia outlining the premises that were guiding its work with four schools located near the University of Georgia. The letter invited schools to send a team consisting of the principal and several teachers to attend a two-day orientation and planning workshop where these premises would be fleshed out.

The workshop reflected the belief that local educators know what is best for their schools. The workshop's purpose was to (1) provide information about the premises that would guide the network's efforts, (2) give school teams an opportunity to reflect on their beliefs about these premises,

(3) share their thoughts with other participants, and (4) help participants consider whether they were interested in implementing these premises in their school and, if so, whether they wanted to pursue membership in a network.

Today, League orientation and planning workshops feature teachers and principals from member schools sharing their experiences in implementing the premises and in networking with other schools. When we ask participants to identify the most helpful part of a workshop, a majority say hearing about the successes, experiences, and challenges that the veteran schools faced.

We know of a network that came to life when a principal, after hearing about the League of Professional Schools, started talking with other teachers and principals in his city about the possibility of forming a network with a similar focus. He received an okay from his central office to move forward with the idea. The U.S. Department of Education's National Diffusion Network gave financial and organizational support to conduct a two-day workshop. Teachers and principals from interested schools met with League staff and practitioners to consider starting a network similar to the League. With a modest budget from their central office, the schools are currently working out what kind of facilitation they want and where they can get it.

Networks don't have to start from scratch. The League is working with an educational agency that has been helping schools for years. The agency thought that some of these schools would benefit from forming a network similar to the League and wanted to find out if their staff were willing to commit to this new type of relationship and if any of the schools were interested in the idea. After a two-day League workshop, participants decided that the agency and the schools had enough interest to start a network. These educators are now ready to meet and determine how their network is going to operate.

Practice What You Preach

The work that goes on under the direction of a network should reflect the premises that the network stands for. For example, a network that is based on democratic premises should take care that those same premises guide the

9

network's activities. A network that supports actively involving students in their own education must be sure to actively involve its participants.

To ensure that a network fulfills its intentions to be practitioner driven, a formal democratic governance process needs to be put in place. If a network operates on an informal, play-it-by-ear basis, its democratic intentions may erode. As people get busy, a tendency to take shortcuts in the decision-making process can lead to autocratic practices without anyone making a conscious decision to undermine the democratic process.

After the first group of schools made a commitment to form a network, the participants established an ad hoc council to develop the type of collaboration that the schools wanted. All schools had a representative on this council: Some provided an administrator; others (the majority), a teacher. This ad hoc council, along with Program for School Improvement staff, selected the name of the collaboration (League of Professional Schools), developed the charter by which the organization would work, and established the membership fee and the services that would be provided. The charter formalized the premises of the League, the conditions in which the collaboration would operate, and the responsibilities of both the League staff and the individual schools. After working in schools sometimes stifled by mandates from the state and the school district, the council was careful to provide an outline on how the network would proceed, rather than lengthy rules and regulations.

Although the member schools don't have the time or inclination to be involved in all the decisions that go into running a network the size of the League, they did want overall control of the direction and the types of activities provided. Toward this end, the council established a Congress of representatives from each League school. To ensure that the Congress represents the schools' populations, two steps are followed to select Congress members. First, each school submits the names of a teacher and an administrator who are willing to serve on the Congress. Second, League staff decide who will serve, based on racial equity, gender equity, and of course keeping teachers in the majority. The Congress reviews the League services annually. Over the years, they've adjusted existing services and added new ones (see Figure 2.1) (see

Chapter 3 for an explanation of these services and Chapter 4 for how the services are evaluated).

The proximity of the schools to each other influences how active a role the practitioners want and can take in the network. For example, networks whose schools are spread over a large geographic area will have more difficulty getting their leadership together frequently. Networks whose schools are not spread out would be able to have a Congress that could meet more often.

Technology can help practitioners more easily govern their network. Teleconferences and electronic mail open up new ways for member schools to discuss issues and make decisions.

Watch Out for the Cookie Cutter

Although we have talked about the strong need for a network to establish an identity based on common beliefs, a network must not expect that all schools implementing its premises will look exactly the same. Network participants must remember the premises that hold them together as a group and also allow and encourage the uniqueness of each school to flourish. The common bonds that make the schools within a network a group should be the parameters. Within these parameters, schools should assume the responsibility of implementing the core premises within the context of their school setting. If schools don't have the ability and expertise to develop their own plan for renewal, then their energy should be centered on building that capacity rather than on following directions from the outside.

Although the League is based on three premises, the manner in which these premises are realized varies from school to school. At the League's first orientation and planning workshop, participants clarified the intent of the premises and the meaning behind them. They used questions to guide team discussions and assist in developing plans for taking this information back to their colleagues. They encouraged the uniqueness of each school and discouraged any idea that the League was promoting a model that all schools should implement.

11

Figure 2.1
Charter for Congress of the
League of Professional Schools

Purpose

The Congress is the official governing body of the League of Professional Schools. In that capacity, the Congress will set the boundaries of League membership, select the basic services all member schools receive, and make decisions concerning League resources (financial and human).

Premises

- The Congress of the League of Professional Schools will adhere to the democratic process both in its representation and mode of operation.
- Representatives of member schools know what is needed to assist their schools to better serve students.
- The League of Professional Schools is an organization where professionals make collective decisions for action and take responsibility for these decisions and actions.
- The League of Professional Schools will be driven by its own internal decisions and criteria of success.

Procedures

1. Each school in the League will submit two candidates for representation on the Congress (one teacher and one administrator from either the school or central office). League staff will select one of these candidates from each school to serve on the Congress. Selection will be based on variety and proportionate representation. Teachers will make up a majority of the Congress. PSI (Program for School Improvement) will have a representative on the Congress.

2. The Congress will determine the budget of the League and the scope of services to be made available to League schools, set League policy, and periodically research and review the value of the League to member schools.

3. A quorum for both the Congress and the Executive Council will consist of a simple majority of total members on each. Decisions for all recommendations must be approved by a two-thirds majority. *Robert's Rules of Order* will guide meeting procedures. Further congressional procedures will be decided upon during the annual conference.

4. The Congress will have an Executive Council. The Executive Council will consist of five teachers, three administrators, and one PSI representative. Members will be chosen by self-nomination. Two pools will be formed, one for teachers and one for administrators, from which names will be randomly selected. The Executive Council will select a chair, cochair, and reporter. These officers will be responsible for (1) introducing resolutions to the Congress, (2) setting the agenda for congressional meetings, (3) clarifying current policies, and (4) meeting with PSI staff to provide guidance as needed. These officers will serve two-year terms.

As specified in the draft charter reviewed by the Congress on October 7, 1990, the Executive Council consists of nine voting members: five teachers, three administrators, and one PSI representative. Names of administrators and teachers who form the Congress were placed in six categories: administrators from (1) elementary, (2) middle, and (3) high school; and teachers from (4) elementary, (5) middle, and (6) high school. One administrator was drawn from each level; three teachers were drawn from the elementary level, one from the middle school level, and one from the high school level.

Scope of Commitment

For a practitioner-driven network to thrive, the member schools must believe that the network will contribute to a better education for their students. The groups of stakeholders (e.g., administrators, teachers, students, parents, and community members) must be committed to the network for the school to be able to fully implement the network's premises. Before a school can take advantage of network membership and make schoolwide changes, a critical mass of the stakeholders should understand the purpose of the school's membership.

Schools must be cautious about always relying on the same group of people for leadership. A small core group working with the network is enough to get the ball rolling, but schools must nurture new interest to build upon the initial momentum. Communication about what is happening and why, frequent dialogue about the network's purpose, and how that purpose can affect the life of the school are essential for building and sustaining enthusiasm. Involving more people, mentoring new participants, and encouraging those on the fringe to get involved must be ongoing activities. The more people who have a broad understanding of what the school is trying to accomplish, the greater the likelihood of success.

After attending the League's orientation and planning workshop, a school team returns to their school and shares what they learned with the entire faculty. The faculty votes about joining the League by secret ballot, which the League requires. Eighty percent must be in favor of the school joining for the school to qualify for membership. We believe that a school must have a majority in favor of doing this type of work if the network is to be successful. For teachers and principals to work together in implementing schoolwide change, they need a strong commitment and belief that the work is worth doing. Once a school joins the League, it can follow its own decision-making process to decide if it wants to continue membership in the League.

A school that does not receive an 80 percent vote is invited to continue discussing whether it should join the League. If the faculty can achieve the votes needed, the school is eligible for membership. Several schools have taken this option and joined, some three years later. By taking the time they needed to build a strong base of support before making this schoolwide commitment, they were able to enter the League with a much greater chance of success in implementing the premises (see Figure 2.2 on p. 15).

Key Points

• Membership in a practitioner-driven network should be voluntary.

• Involving school teams in network activities from the beginning helps create an atmosphere of reflection, collegiality, and teamwork.

• Before joining a network, the stakeholders need a thorough understanding of the network's guiding premises.

• The people whom a network is supposed to help should control the activities of the network from the beginning.

• Network governance processes should be fully developed, recorded, and publicized so that everyone knows them and can use them.

• Network governance bodies should represent the people participating in a network.

• Schools joining a network do not need to implement the network's premises in the same way. The uniqueness of each school must be recognized.

• A school should not join a network unless a majority of the educators in the school agree to the affiliation.

Figure 2.2
Membership Application for the League of Professional Schools

_____   _____
      Name of School   Contact Person

School Commitment

We have reviewed the process of shared governance with our faculty. At least 80 percent have agreed to participate in the Program for School Improvement (PSI) League of Professional Schools.

We are committed to establishing representative, democratic decision-making procedures. We support teacher involvement in schoolwide instructional decisions. School system authorities are aware of and supportive of our partnership with the PSI League of Professional Schools and our intention to use shared governance to bring about instructional improvement at _____ School.

We agree to set and work collectively on attaining school instructional goals. Data will be collected to assess our progress and to determine the effects of various activities on teachers and students. We are willing to share our experience with colleagues in other schools by receiving guests in our school and through presentations.

PSI League of Professional Schools Commitment

PSI League members will receive through their affiliation with the League

1. Assistance with action plans at follow-up meetings to be held at central locations.

2. A PSI League of Professional Schools network exchange newsletter.

3. An information retrieval system to honor requests for information relevant to instructional initiatives.

4. Planning, evaluation, research, and instrumentation services via telephone.

5. An annual League conference.

6. One on-site visit by PSI League staff.

_____
Name

_____
Date

3
The Work

IN A PRACTITIONER-DRIVEN NETWORK, THE NETWORK FACILITATOR'S
main functions are to help schools stay focused on the
network's premises, foster across-school communication,
help create a nonhierarchical climate that values
collaboration, and infuse the network with information and
resources. This chapter discusses guidelines, services, and
activities that the facilitator can provide to help the
network serve these functions. Not all network facilitators
will have the resources to provide all the services; networks
will need to operate with services that fit their unique needs
and resources.

Meeting Preparation

Preparing for network meetings first requires answering
where, what, and who questions: Where should the meeting
be held? What is the meeting for? What needs to be on the
agenda? Who should be involved?

Picking a Meeting Site

We recommend holding meetings in as pleasant,
well-appointed a site as a network's budget will allow. Sites
that provide aesthetically pleasing meeting rooms with
comfortable seating, good sound systems, excellent
refreshments, and meals establish a professional climate
well worth the price. Such accommodations tell the
participants that they are appreciated and create an
expectation of excellence. As a teacher explained after
attending a League meeting: "I loved the way we were

treated. We were at a beautiful place, and the meeting was run with a professionalism that I don't think we're used to."

Geographic location is another consideration. When schools in a network are geographically spread out, the network's governing body should consider meeting in different locations to provide equitable access to all schools. Seemingly small issues can sometimes create perceptions of favoritism and undermine the network's efforts.

Setting Agendas

Meeting agendas should reflect what the schools want. A number of activities can help facilitators ensure meetings are on target:

• Obtain input through the network's governing body and surveys that give schools the opportunity to indicate their wishes for upcoming meetings.

• Listen continually to the schools so that meetings incorporate the concerns and issues the schools face.

• Form a task force or committee of representatives from the schools to work with the network staff in creating meeting agendas.

• Give participants opportunities to evaluate meetings, and make sure that future meetings reflect their wishes.

School Teams

Network meetings should involve school teams, not individuals, representing a school. Teams give more people firsthand experience in the network and provide a model for reflection and collaborative school planning. Participating as a team also creates an atmosphere that encourages a different level of responsibility from that of participating as an individual. Being a team member emphasizes that participants are to act as a representative of the school, not as an individual. The team has the responsibility of returning to school and sharing new information and suggestions for next steps with other faculty members so that the entire school benefits from the meeting.

17

Including a variety of people on the teams is also important. Many schools send two or three members to attend most of the League meetings, providing continuity to their work, and rotate other faculty members who attend. They find this arrangement broadens the depth of their involvement with the League and keeps the team from becoming alienated from the rest of their colleagues.

Meeting Formats and Activities

Preparation and top rate accommodations can't make up for meetings that are poorly conceived, planned, and executed. Practitioner-driven network meetings should demonstrate the values of collaborative reflection and encourage building the schools' competence in serving students rather than building the expertise of a chosen few.

Opportunities for Reflection

Meetings that feature a keynote speaker should include time for school teams to reflect on what the speaker has said and to discuss the implications for their school. This time gives participants an opportunity to hear and express concurring and dissenting points of view and reinforces the idea that everyone's voice is important. It also stresses to participants that they are attending meetings as representatives of their school and not just for their own professional edification. Taking ideas back to schools and sharing so that everyone has access to the information are critical for schools to develop a schoolwide focus.

Breakout Sessions

Practitioner-driven network meetings should generally have practitioners as featured parts of the agenda. Member schools should have a standing invitation to submit proposals for presentations. Concurrent breakout sessions are an effective way to highlight what schools are doing. Not only does this opportunity for sharing provide information to participants, but it also prompts the presenting school to take a fresh look at what its faculty is doing. Such a review may provide the school with a cause for celebration and help identify the next step.

We encourage teams to split up and attend different breakout sessions so that they can hear many new ideas. Later in the meeting, they need to be given an opportunity to share what they have learned. To help teams decide what sessions to attend, the agenda should include a summary of what will be covered in each breakout session.

Featuring Schools Outside the Network

To infuse a network with new ideas and ways of doing things, some meetings should highlight teams from schools outside the network. Network facilitators and practitioners should constantly be on the lookout for exemplary schools that have undertaken work of interest to schools in the network.

Sharing

A group of people sitting together in a large room does not necessarily help them in getting to know and learn from each other. Time needs to be set aside to allow schools to share with other schools what they are doing and the lessons they are learning and to discuss issues that concern them.

An activity called Discoveries has successfully facilitated across-school sharing at League meetings. Although the focus of discoveries sessions varies from meeting to meeting, we have found one question that works well with any focus: "What is your school doing that you are particularly proud of?" School teams are given a few minutes to discuss their thoughts among themselves, using the session's focus as the frame of reference; then the session leader asks individuals to find a person who is not on their team to share their team's response. Each person has a discovery sheet for notes, phone numbers, and names of colleagues from other schools. To facilitate sharing, name tags with colored dots indicating whether the wearer is from a high, middle, or elementary school are provided.

On the leader's signal, participants return to their teams. This is usually a difficult task because people invariably get so involved in sharing that they don't want to stop. The reassembled teams are given time to share what each member discovered. The discoveries activity usually whets the appetites of those involved, initiating ongoing, across-school collaborations and stimulating school team thinking.

Team Planning Time

Lack of time is a major barrier to schools taking collective, thoughtful action. A typical school day doesn't include time for collaborative reflection, discussions, or planning. Consequently, a block of time for individual teams to work on their own agenda is a critical part of network meetings. Teams can discuss how they will share their experiences with the rest of the faculty or how to develop, assess, and revise their future plans. These activities reinforce that the team's attendance at meetings is expected to affect their school.

Practitioner-driven networks can also legitimize people taking time to talk about their work away from the hustle and bustle of the school. League colleagues tell us that even if they had arrived at a meeting to find it had been canceled, the time together in the drive to and from the meeting was appreciated and helpful.

Figure 3.1 is an example of a typical League meeting agenda. Notice the time for reflection and celebration in the morning, the breakout sessions, the time for across-school sharing in the afternoon, and team planning time.

Action Plans

Schools are busy places, with so many demands made on the faculty that even the most well-intentioned educators sometimes have trouble moving from talking about doing something to actually doing it. Practitioner-driven networks can use action plans to assist member schools in getting started and in following through. An action plan calls for a school to set goals and identify hoped-for results and strategies that will be used to attain outcomes. Then comes the critical part. An action plan should include the activities needed to realize the school's goals, a time line for when the activities will occur, the persons responsible for each activity, the resources and

Figure 3.1
Meeting Agenda

8:30–9:00 a.m.	Registration
9:00–9:15 a.m.	Welcome, Introductions, Announcements
9:15–10:00 a.m.	Reflection and Celebration
10:00–10:20 a.m.	Break
10:20–11:00 a.m.	Breakout Session 1

Room 1 **Grant Writing**
Douglas County High
Overview of the responsibilities, problems, and pitfalls of grant writing, including locating sources, writing the outline, and the review process.

Room 2 **Ninth Grade Success Program**
Duluth High
Describes a program on how to provide a successful transition from middle school to high school. Teams of four teachers teach 9th grade students.

Room 3 **Parental Involvement in Shared Governance**
Herschel Jones Middle School
Members of the Jones Middle School's coordinating council, including two parents, discuss parental involvement in shared governance. Focuses on (1) the decision to include parents on the council and how conflicts were resolved; (2) reaction from parents and the importance of their input; and (3) continuation and increase in parental involvement.

Room 4 **Mathematics Across the Curriculum: An Eisenhower Grant**
Center Junior High
Focuses on (1) the rationale for project-based interdisciplinary units; (2) ideas gained from implementing the grant and the grant's utilization in the school; and (3) suggestions for writing Eisenhower math/science grants.

Room 5 **Conversations About Authentic Assessment**
Georgia State Department of Education
Overview of NCREST (National Center for Restructuring Education, Schools, and Teaching) conference visit, description of NCREST, and an example of a program using authentic assessment with NCREST support. Concludes with group interaction describing types of authentic assessments currently used in the League.

Room 6 **Conversations with Principals**
League Staff
Explores the critical issues of shared governance and action research in a roundtable discussion. Session is for principals interested in sharing their experiences with other principals.

**Figure 3.1—*continued*
Meeting Agenda**

11:05–11:45 a.m.   *Breakout Session 2*

Room 1   **Grant Writing**
Douglas County High
Overview of the responsibilities, problems, and pitfalls of grant
writing, including locating sources, writing the outline, and the
review process.

Room 2   **Ninth Grade Success Program**
Duluth High
Describes a program on how to provide a successful transition
from middle school to high school. Teams of four teachers teach
9th grade students.

Room 3   **School Within a School: The House Plan**
Conyers Middle
A plan that was originally designed to allow the school to better
serve at-risk students has evolved into a comprehensive
restructuring effort. The House Plan is based on research on
creating effective programs for at-risk students.

Room 4   **Mathematics Across the Curriculum: An Eisenhower
Grant**
Center Junior High
Focuses on (1) the rationale for project-based interdisciplinary
units; (2) ideas gained from implementing the grant and the grant's
utilization in the school; and (3) suggestions for writing
Eisenhower math/science grants.

Room 5   **Conversations About Authentic Assessment**
Georgia State Department of Education
Overview of NCREST conference visit, description of NCREST,
and an example of a program using authentic assessment with
NCREST support. Concludes with group interaction describing
types of authentic assessments currently used in the League.

Room 6   **Conversations with Teachers**
League Staff
Explores the critical issues of shared governance and action
research in a roundtable discussion. Session is for teachers
interested in sharing their experiences with others.

11:45 a.m.–1:15 p.m.	Lunch and Team Preparation for Discoveries
1:15–2:15 p.m.	Discoveries
2:15–2:40 p.m.	Team Sharing
2:40–3:00 p.m.	Closing Remarks

assistance that will be needed, and a process or procedure to determine if the school has accomplished its goals. The school should be responsible for setting the plan's focus and the strategies it will use to implement the plan. The most important part of an action plan is just doing it! It must not be just another exercise in paperwork that has no real meaning to what happens each day with students and teachers.

The League asks that each school submit an action plan. To help ensure that the plan will be a working document that fits the school's needs, schools are encouraged to use various formats. If a school's district also requires an action plan, we suggest the school use that format. If a school has designed its own action plan format, that's fine, too. The plan's format or appearance is not important—its content and implementation are.

A pitfall we all face with action plans is the twice-a-year syndrome: We look at our plan twice a year, once when we write it and later when we report on our progress. League meetings, held every three months throughout the school year, include time for a school team to review their school's action plan, reflect on their progress, identify problem areas, celebrate accomplishments, and decide their next steps. At every League meeting, we include in a school team's meeting materials a copy of their plan. Schools tell us that having this opportunity to review and reflect, away from the daily demands of school, is most helpful and a true luxury.

Using carbonless paper for these plans allows the network facilitator to have a copy. Knowing what action plans the schools are working on helps the facilitator in planning meetings and services (see Figure 3.2).

Institutes

Daylong or multiday institutes permit teams to explore a single topic in more depth than can be done in a meeting format. Topics are chosen from network staff observations, informal conversations with teachers and principals, on-site visit summaries (more on these later), and a formal survey. Although schools send teams to an institute site, teams may use the time as a retreat where they follow their own

Figure 3.2
Action Plan Format

School _____ Date _____

Contact Person _____ Phone No. _____

1. Goal: What is the greatest priority of instructional improvement that the school can act upon for the next several years? (You may have more than one.)

2. What are the hoped-for results for students?

3. What other results might occur?

4. What strategy or strategies will be used to attain student outcomes?

5. If you are dealing with more than one goal, how do they relate?

Action Plan

School _____ Date _____

Activities	Target Date	Person(s) Responsible	Resources/ Assistance	Assessment/ Outcomes

agenda rather than participating in a preplanned program. Team members can then interact with staff who are not involved in the formal agenda during the day and with other institute participants in the evenings.

The League holds its institutes in the summer. Schools prefer this time because they can send large numbers of teachers for several days without the teachers being away from their students. Offering staff development and continuing education credits for interested teachers is also beneficial.

Information Retrieval System

Information that pertains to a network's focus is a vital service that a network facilitator should consider providing to member schools. Facilitators not in a position to provide this service may be able to contract it out to an agency. Schools typically don't have the time or resources to thoroughly research issues or to stay informed about what other schools are doing. By providing schools with information, a network can help them make informed decisions.

An information retrieval system can offer schools both resource-based information and literature-based information. The first refers to people or organizations that can act as resources to schools. In a practitioner-driven network, an important source of resource-based information is the other schools in the network. For example, if a school contacts the network wanting more information about Issue A, the network should be able to provide the names of member schools that are also working on Issue A. We are not implying that a network should have the capability to supply schools with resources found only within the network. An information retrieval system should be able to provide schools with diverse resource possibilities.

As schools become aware of different instructional approaches or techniques, they will need literature-based information to decide if they want to do anything about what they've learned. Let's continue with the example of Issue A. After fleshing out the exact nature of information the school wants about Issue A, the network provides the school with a packet of information containing journal articles; cases studies from other network schools; books; research reports; papers; and videos, including videos of presentations made at network meetings. Because time for reading is short, the packets should contain about five to eight pieces of information.

This type of service is greatly appreciated and helps infuse the network with new ideas. Such a service demonstrates the network's belief that information is vital to the success of the collaboration. Networks are not only for sharing the expertise found in the participating schools but also for providing information to schools from a broad base of sources.

The League's Information Retrieval Service doesn't limit the number of searches a school can request; it does stipulate, however, that requests must be schoolwide and signed by a representative of the school's decision-making body. The League doesn't have the resources to provide searches for individual teachers. The League pledges to respond within 10 working days.

On-Site Visits

School-based educators sometimes gets so close to their work that they may have difficulty looking at it to determine whether they are satisfied with what they see. Issues may need to be put on the table, but nobody knows quite how to go about it. Experienced, perceptive colleagues, not directly involved in a school's work, can often assist by visiting the school and providing it with a look at itself through a different lens. These on-site facilitators may ask questions or offer suggestions to help the school in its review; they should not issue verdicts about whether the school's work measures up. The people in the school make any needed judgments.

The League has learned some key lessons about on-site visits:

• Teachers and principals make excellent on-site facilitators. Practitioners make over 50 percent of the League's on-site visits, and the percent increases yearly.

• Teachers and principals are usually skeptical about someone coming into their school "to help," which often gets translated into "someone is coming into our school to judge whether we are 'doing it right.'" Networks need to be sensitive to this perception. Facilitators need to make sure they explain that they are there to listen and learn, not to judge. They will need to say this type of statement more than once, and they must make sure they do exactly what they say!

• Individuals, pairs, or teams can make the annual visits. In the beginning stages of a practitioner-driven network, network staff may need to conduct the on-site visits. But practitioners should begin making visits as soon as they have gained enough experience. Eventually, practitioners should make a majority of the visits. Schools receiving the visits benefit from contact with colleagues who have a close understanding of the working conditions, and practitioners making the visit benefit from hearing what other schools are doing. New networks that want on-site visits but don't yet feel their staff have the expertise to make them may be able to work with an established network.

• A network's leadership should work out the procedures for the visits. If interviews will be conducted, interview questions should be carefully thought out. Following the same general format helps a network make generalizations across schools (see Figure 3.3).

• On-site facilitators should write a summary of their visit to give to the school and to the network facilitator. A summary acts as a mirror to the school, giving people in the school access to the on-site facilitators' reflections. By analyzing summaries from all the member schools, the network facilitator can get an across-school understanding about how schools are feeling about their work and how the network can help (more on evaluation in Chapter 6; see Appendix for an on-site visit summary).

• On-site visits should focus only on the network's focus. They shouldn't be wide-ranging visits that look at all aspects of the school's activities.

Figure 3.3
Procedure for On-Site Visits

1. Guided walk through the school to gain a sense of students, teachers, organization for teaching, and teaching (*30 minutes*).

2. Interviews with the following people:*

    a. Principal (*30 minutes*)

    b. Chair of governing board (*30 minutes*)

    c. Two teachers: one who has taken an active role in the school's involvement with the League of Professional Schools and one who has taken a less active role (*30 minutes each*).

    d. One group of four to five students from different grades (*30 minutes*).

3. Review of relevant materials from chair or principal (e.g., memos, letters, announcements, charters, constitutions, and school plans).

4. Group discussion with the school's shared leadership group to provide an opportunity to ask questions; share their expertise; provide feedback to PSI and the League Congress concerning League procedures and services; and update and clarify any information needed to enhance our collaboration (*30 minutes*).

5. Spend the remainder of the day doing what the school thinks is important.

*Before the visit, a school-based person needs to schedule the interviews. Interviewees should be volunteers who represent the school's socioeconomic and ethnic makeup. Assure the interviewees that what they say will be confidential and that notes will be used only to summarize the school's improvement efforts; they will not identify any individual. Interviews may be tape recorded if permission is granted by the interviewee.

• Schools should be given the final voice in who visits. Facilitators should not be assigned without a school's approval.

When League facilitators make on-site visits, they follow a set procedure unless the school requests otherwise. Time is built in to the procedure if the school wants to customize it. School-based educators can also rearrange the plan to better fit their needs.

The League sees on-site visits as a critical service to schools. New on-site facilitators are carefully taken through the procedure and interview questions before they make their visits. Also, special attention is given to writing the on-site summaries. We give new facilitators samples of on-site summaries that include the information and the tone that schools have found most helpful. To further ensure that these summaries provide the appropriate type of information and take a collegial, nonjudgmental tone, new facilitators are asked to have an experienced facilitator review them before they are given to schools. In fact, most experienced facilitators continue to get a second opinion on summaries before sending them out. This practice helps avoid hurt feelings and misunderstandings.

Key Points

- Network meetings should establish the tone and climate for a collaboration; therefore, they should model a network's values.
- In a practitioner-driven network, practitioners should have a strong voice in setting meeting agendas.
- In a practitioner-driven network, practitioners sharing their expertise should be at the heart of all network meetings.
- A network must constantly be infused with outside information.
- A critical function of networks is to help schools take and sustain action.
- Network membership is an ongoing involvement that builds over time.

4
Ongoing Issues

BECAUSE THEY ARE SO INTERACTIVE AND PERSON ORIENTED,
practitioner-driven networks are fragile and require
constant care. A smooth-running network needs ongoing
maintenance to stay that way. Issues and relationships must
constantly be monitored and addressed.

Focus

The longer a network exists, the more diverse the
member schools' needs will become. New schools join and
others drop out. Some move ahead with implementing the
premises relatively quickly and need help in refining their
work and looking for creative ways to expand what they are
doing. Others move slower and continue to need help with
basic issues. The challenge is to provide services that
continue to be on target for the needs of all schools while
keeping a common focus.

For a network to stay focused, people need to
repeatedly tell the network's story. Meetings, newsletters,
on-site visits, and informal discussions can periodically
recap why the network was started, chronicle key events,
put the network's work in context with that of other
networks or similar organizations, share the lessons that
have been learned, celebrate accomplishments, and create
exciting expectations for the future. People need frequent
boosts to their sense of community and common purpose
to stay focused over the long run.

 When a new group of schools joins the League, we
have a meeting expressly for them. We give the schools
information about how the League was started, how it

works, and how to take advantage of its services. We share what they can expect to happen when they start doing this work. Faculty members from veteran schools (League members for at least two years) explain how they have gone about implementing the premises, what pitfalls to avoid, and what the new schools should be sure to do. This sharing is valuable not only to the new schools but also to the schools making the presentations; it helps them rethink what they are doing and why.

Most information given at the new-member meeting is similar to that presented at the orientation and planning meeting, but schools need to hear it again even if the same team attended both meetings. We have learned that information needs to be presented several times in different ways before it is fully grasped by a high percentage of the people in a school. School-based educators need opportunities to apply new knowledge in their work setting before they can gain a personal understanding of a concept. To assume that information covered in one meeting doesn't need to be mentioned again is a mistake. People frequently say to us after they have attended several meetings, "The light just came on. Now I really understand what you have been talking about. For the first time I see the possibilities of what we are all trying to do." A network is much more likely to keep its focus if its members have a thorough understanding of the network's premises.

Most meetings have breakout sessions that cover the League's premises and services. About one-fourth of the participants are attending their first meeting. Schools use these sessions to introduce more staff to what the League's work is—a never-ending task in schools where new teachers are arriving and veterans moving on.

At a League meeting general session, network staff recap how and why the League was started and give a progress report about what has been accomplished. This update doesn't have to take long; 15 to 20 minutes has proven sufficient. But without it, we would lose our image of who we are and what we are doing.

Feedback on Services

Practitioner-driven networks should constantly seek feedback on the services they provide member schools. Networks need this to make adjustments, not so they can be judged good or bad.

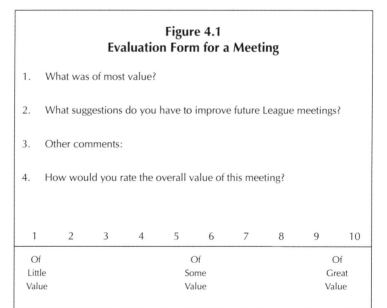

• *Evaluation forms* provide feedback about League meetings (see Figure 4.1). The forms produce both qualitative information from open-ended questions and quantitative information from a Likert scale. Responses are summarized and carefully studied. Such a practice has helped the League fine-tune its meetings so that they continue to be well received year after year.

Figure 4.1
Evaluation Form for a Meeting

1.   What was of most value?

2.   What suggestions do you have to improve future League meetings?

3.   Other comments:

4.   How would you rate the overall value of this meeting?

1	2	3	4	5	6	7	8	9	10

Of Little Value	Of Some Value	Of Great Value

• *On-site visits* are evaluated to provide continuous feedback about their value. Schools complete an evaluation form that helps the League staff and schools decide who will make future visits (see Figure 4.2); and a facilitator interview question asks how the League's services are affecting the schools.

Figure 4.2
Evaluation Form for an On-Site Visit

School Name _____

1. List the aspect of the on-site visit that you found to be the most helpful to your school.

2. What part(s) of the visit would you prefer to have changed for next year?

3. Was the amount of time the facilitator spent in your school appropriate to your needs? If no, please explain.

4. Please indicate your needs for next year:

    _____We would like to have the same facilitator return to our school next year.

    _____We would like a new facilitator for next year. We would like this facilitator to have expertise in the following area(s):

    _____

    We would like our PSI facilitator to be
    _____ from the university
    _____ a practitioner from a League school
    _____ either—we have no preference

    _____ We are open to either having the same facilitator return or a different facilitator.

5. For us, the on-site summary was . . . . (*please describe*)

Comments/Suggestions:

- *Annual telephone interviews* provide information that has led to meaningful changes in League services.

Handling Uncommitted Schools

What do you do with a school that is not making a good faith commitment to implement the network's premises and is taking up a membership slot that another school might make better use of? Networks that charge an annual membership fee are less likely to have this problem, but it can still happen.

The network's governance body will need to address this issue. We recommend a policy that specifies a minimum participation requirement so that schools not attending meetings or using the services will be dropped from the network, after extended communication with the network's leadership. Schools that are members in name only do not benefit the network. Membership should imply that a school is actively pursuing a course of action, not just enjoying the prestige that comes with the association.

Reaching Out

Networks, like schools, should not work in isolation. When networks seek other organizations that are doing similar work and create collaborative lines of communication with them, they put themselves in a position to learn and grow in their understanding of how to promote the work of their member schools. Some networks will have resources to send people to visit other organizations to pick up new ideas and stretch their thinking; others will need to find less expensive ways to reach out.

The League routinely sends staff and practitioners to visit other organizations so that they can share what they learned at League meetings. We also send people to conferences and workshops, with two charges: Learn things that will help your school, and be alert for schools and organizations that the League can learn from.

When other educators interested in our work contact the League, we try to respond to their request. Because school-based people are so active in the League, we have many who are able to tell the League's story; thus, we have a large capacity to reach out to others. Teachers and principals from League schools have made presentations throughout the United States and Canada. Schools have benefited from this experience because faculty members return excited and refreshed. Plus, they usually bring back good ideas for the schools to consider.

League schools also receive many visitors and respond positively to requests. They see these visits as an opportunity to reflect on their work, and they find that visitors have information and experiences that can help a school's work.

Growth

How big should a practitioner-driven network get? How fast should a network grow? By now, you probably won't be surprised that our answer is "It's up to the schools in the network." Because practitioner-driven networks rely on teachers and principals feeling comfortable in seeking and exchanging information and forming across-school relationships, and because services and information need to be provided promptly, the number of schools in the network should not get too large. On the other hand, only a few schools in a network limit the diversity of perspectives available to members.

During its first year, the League had 22 schools. By the end of that year, we felt comfortable with each other. Meetings were characterized by people greeting each other by name and feeling at home. Room arrangements were easy because we didn't need much space. Working with only a few schools meant fewer things to go wrong, fewer phone calls to make, and fewer personalities that were expected to mesh.

The second year, 23 more schools joined after attending the orientation and planning workshop and obtaining the required 80 percent vote. Two original schools dropped their membership. At this point, the League Congress debated what to do about future growth. They discussed the value of bringing in new schools with fresh ideas versus getting so big that

35

meetings might lose their homey feel. They decided that the League should grow no larger than 60 schools. Consequently, the third year, we followed a pattern that was similar to that of the first two years, and the League stood at 60 schools.

The League has profited from bringing in new schools—fresh perspectives, ideas, approaches to instruction, and energy. Each year, as a few schools drop out, we bring in new schools, never exceeding the 60-school guideline. During the League's fourth year, the idea of breaking schools into geographical regions surfaced. A proposal called for the League to stay intact but for schools to be able to network regionally. The League Congress rejected the idea. They highly valued mixing with schools from across the state and were not interested in spending time in regional activities that might restrict the member schools' diversity. Each year, however, more schools are forming alliances within the League. These arrangements do not replace the schools' participation in the League; they are in addition to them. Another type of networking is a possibility: networking by grade level. For example, League middle schools may want to do something together. This type of arrangement may appeal to many schools, but the question they ask is "When will we find time to attend regular League meetings and these other meetings as well?" Some sort of network-within-a-larger-network would be a viable option for networks that have grown to include many schools and span a large geographical area.

Key Points

- For a network to build and maintain its focus, its members need a deep understanding of its basic premises.
- A network must continually articulate why it was formed, how it operates, and where it is headed.
- A network must constantly evaluate its effects on schools and make adjustments accordingly.
- To maintain its integrity, a network must insist that its members operate in good faith to implement its premises.
- For a network to improve, it should interact with other organizations and networks that have a similar focus and operating procedures.
- A network should reflect about its growth. Its size should be consistent with its purpose.

5
The Action Research Consortium

NETWORKS CAN CREATE FACILITATIVE AND LEADERSHIP ROLES FOR
school-based educators—roles that offer professional
opportunities usually available only for those based outside
schools, such as central office staff, university faculty, and
private consultants. The League's Action Research
Consortium (ARC) exemplifies how practitioners can be
actively involved in the professional work of a
practitioner-driven network. The consortium provides
member schools with access to school-based consultants
who have the experience, professional background, and
expertise to help schools move forward. And to those
taking on the new roles, the consortium provides
professional experiences that enhance their school-based
work, thus keeping the energy where it is needed most—in
the schools.

How ARC Was Formed

At a summer retreat, League staff were reviewing what
had been accomplished to date and what should be the
focus of the upcoming school year. On-site visit summaries
and informal interactions with our colleagues clearly
indicated that schools were not as far along with their
action research efforts as they wanted to be. The questions
then were "What help do they want? What is the best way to
deliver it?" We realized we were not qualified to answer
these questions, even though League staff spend many
hours in member schools and work closely with the schools
in the activities that bring us all together.

We decided to invite seven or eight teachers and principals from a variety of schools to spend an afternoon with us brainstorming what the League's strategy should be. Named the Ad Hoc Action Research Committee, the group met at a centrally located League school. The League reimbursed participants for expenses and gave them a stipend for their time.

Committee members discussed their efforts to conduct action research; the effectiveness of the help that the League offered; possible modifications to existing services; and additional services that may be needed. They agreed that the current practice of providing meeting sessions that focused on different aspects of action research was helpful and should be continued. They also agreed that some schools needed something more. Some members felt frustrated by the indifference shown when they tried to share their excitement and new insights from action research sessions with colleagues who hadn't attended a meeting. What was needed was a way to get as many school-based educators as possible to hear the same information at the same time. Much was being lost in translation when meeting participants tried to take information back to their colleagues.

The committee thought that all would benefit from having experts in action research come to their schools, listen to their concerns, and provide the specific information and coaching needed to move forward. Such a plan would eliminate the problem of a few people trying to pass a message along to many colleagues.

Members then asked the question "Where would we find such expertise?" The answer was "In League schools." Committee members agreed that they should invite individuals to consider joining the Action Research Consortium (ARC), a group to lead the League's efforts in facilitating action research. Consortium members should be working in veteran League schools, having some success in action research, and interested in working closely with other League schools. League staff would assist ARC members in designing professional development activities, operating procedures, and service delivery models.

The League sent a letter to the member schools that were in at least their second year of League membership.

The letter outlined ARC's purpose and invited those who were interested and thought they fit the description to attend a two-day meeting to create the consortium. Ten teachers and an assistant principal responded. Luckily, elementary, middle, and high schools were all represented. If they had not been, we would have encouraged schools from the missing levels to send a representative.

Setting up ARC

At the first ARC meeting, League staff summarized how the Ad Hoc Action Research Committee had been formed and what the committee hoped ARC would accomplish. After introductions and discussion about the experiences each member brought to the group, members chose a chair.

Participants shared ideas on how they could best facilitate schools' action research efforts and reviewed what was and wasn't working in their own schools. With the help of League staff taking detailed notes, ARC developed a list of problems and successes. Using experiences in their own schools as sounding boards, the committee outlined various strategies that could be used in working with schools. League staff recorded and organized the discussion.

On the second day, participants formed five groups. Group 1 worked on developing guiding objectives for ARC; Group 2 discussed what materials were needed for working with schools; Group 3 brainstormed possible formats for working with schools (e.g., entire faculty, small groups, half-day, and full day); Group 4 created an evaluation instrument for when ARC members provided a service; and Group 5 identified strategies for making schools aware of ARC and what it could provide them.

Finally, the committee agreed on when they should meet again and what the next meeting's purpose would be. They decided to invite two university-based researchers to share experiences in collecting and analyzing data. ARC members would again share their experiences as they continued to expand work in their schools.

A League meeting featured ARC members sharing what they had been doing to prepare themselves to be action research facilitators and the different types of services they could offer. Others with the appropriate background were invited to join the consortium.

ARC operated informally for the first year, then created bylaws to guide the work. Facilitators share the lessons they learn when working with schools and refining ARC's methods. In short, they are growing in their ability to work in their own schools and in other schools. ARC members have made numerous presentations at League meetings and at other professional meetings throughout the United States. Membership has roughly doubled from the original number and continues to be open to all League schools.

Finances

PSI secured a grant to finance ARC activities. Most grant money that a university receives is used to create opportunities and additional resources for those who work in the university. ARC serves as a model for how grant money can be used to directly expand the work of school-based educators.

ARC money finances the professional development of its members in many ways:

• Substitute pay and traveling expenses for members attending sessions.

• Outside expertise.

• Books, videotapes, and other materials.

• Stipends, substitute pay, and traveling expenses for members making school presentations; and substitute pay for those wanting to meet with an ARC facilitator. Generally, a facilitator meets with an entire faculty during student-free workdays.

The structure of school-based educators' workdays makes taking on professional roles outside of school difficult. Using grant money to break this isolation is a powerful way to help schools help themselves.

The Role of PSI

PSI plays an important but unobtrusive role; ARC decides what that role is:

• Make arrangements for meeting dates and work with cochairs in planning the meetings.

• Participate in meetings.

• Ensure that members have the materials they need for working with schools (e.g., overheads, handouts, and guidebooks).

• Act as treasurer. Reimburse members for expenses and stipends and buy needed materials. ARC establishes the guidelines on how to spend the money.

• Act as secretary. Take meeting minutes and provide each member with a copy.

• Act as a clearinghouse for services. Schools that want help from ARC contact PSI, who matches a school's needs with the ARC member(s) best suited to meet the needs.

Key Points

• Providing structures to help practitioners who are taking leadership roles increases the likelihood that a network will offer services that reflect what the member schools want and will use.

• Summarizing key information from dialogues and presenting it in easy-to-digest form, such as lists, short statements, and graphs, can help meeting participants organize their thoughts.

• The skills and experiences that practitioners develop when they help other schools enhance their own school-based work.

• School-based educators have little time to take on professional roles outside of schools. Consequently, when a school requests professional expertise, financial resources are usually used to bring in outside help. Grant money can be used to build the capacity of teachers and principals so that they can help each other.

6
Evaluating a Network

IN ADDITION TO OBTAINING FEEDBACK ON ITS SERVICES (SEE
Chapter 4), a network needs to ask two questions to
evaluate its overall work: How are the member schools
progressing in implementing the network's premises? Do
the network practices reflect the premises under which the
network was founded?

To help answer these questions, we have identified
four basic activities that a network can undertake to
evaluate its effect on member schools. We offer our
methods as a menu of possibilities that should be modified
to fit a network's situation:

- Analyze actions that schools take over time.
- Study schools' participation patterns in using a
network's services.
- Interview school-based educators about their work
with a network's premises and analyze their responses.
- Encourage schools to study and write about their
experiences with a network.

On-site visits can play an important part in an
evaluation process. Written summaries provide information
that allows a network to analyze schools' actions, and the
visits provide opportunities to interview people, generating
more detailed information. We think on-site visits are
essential for a network to evaluate its effects on member
schools. The League's model of using teachers and
principals to conduct these visits and write summaries (see
Chapter 3) enables any size network to provide visits to all
participants.

Analyzing Actions

Analyzing a school's actions can show how the school implements changes. Studying these actions over time can reveal patterns that give a network a sense of whether member schools are headed in the desired direction. What is counted and compared will vary, depending on a network's focus. For example, a network that believes students should not be separated for instructional purposes could count and compare over time the number of students in member schools who are segregated for these purposes. We'd hope they would see the numbers diminishing.

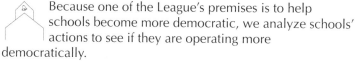 Because one of the League's premises is to help schools become more democratic, we analyze schools' actions to see if they are operating more democratically.

In the League's first year, principals appointed 25 percent of the teachers who were in leadership positions. This practice steadily decreased, and by the fifth year, none of the schools had appointed leaders; they either volunteered or were elected. We believe this decrease showed that schools were operating more democratically than when the League began.

Another study compared the number of school leadership teams that principals chaired to the number of leadership teams that an elected leader chaired. Over five years, the number of leadership teams that principals have chaired has dwindled to zero.

An additional sign that teachers are taking on new school roles is that teachers, not principals, are signing more of the school's annual letters of commitment to the League.

Perhaps the strongest evidence that schools are becoming more democratic is how schools define who is eligible to serve on leadership teams. In the early years, nearly all schools used only certified staff. Five years later, over 50 percent of the leadership teams include students, parents, and noncertified staff.

Examining who makes the annual on-site visits provides an indicator of whether the League is following its intentions to increase practitioner involvement in the League's work. In the 1990–91 school year, League staff or university associates made all on-site visits. In the 1991–92 school year, teachers and principals made 2 percent of the visits. The percent has increased each year. In the 1994–95 school year, practitioners are scheduled to make over 50 percent of the visits.

The most visible action a school can take is to drop from the League. Not renewing a membership is not necessarily a sign that a school is unhappy with its affiliation. Sometimes a school decides that the League has taken it as far as the League can, and the school is ready to operate on its own. Others find different affiliations that more closely match actions they want to pursue. We have not found any pattern in the number of schools that have chosen not to renew their membership; an equal number of secondary and elementary schools have dropped—some from rural areas, some suburban, and some urban. Eighty-four percent of the schools that originally joined the League are still members. Considering the amount of resources needed for schools to participate in the League, we believe this percentage is a sign of a healthy network. Continuously tracking these numbers will alert us to developing membership trends.

Participation Patterns in Using Services

Studying how and how often schools use a network's services can show a link between a school's success in implementing the network's premises and the school's participation in the network. Participation patterns can also indicate how schools can best use a network's services and how those services might need to be modified to better help schools.

 We have learned that schools who report success in implementing the League's premises almost always send a full team of six to League meetings. Consequently, a school that misses a meeting or only sends two or three people alerts us to finding out why. The school may be experiencing a difficulty for which it needs some assistance.

At all League meetings, we ask that team members complete a sign-in sheet. Such a procedure allows us to keep track of who is attending: Are schools sending the same people to all meetings? Are they sending a new team each time? Are they sending a combination of experienced and first-time members? By comparing attendance information with that about schools' successes in implementing the League's premises, we noted a link between a high level of implementation and a school's tendency to send a team that consisted of veterans and first-time members.

We used this information in two ways. First, we increased from four to six the number of team members that schools are allowed to send to meetings. Second, we shared the information with member schools, and many are now making greater efforts to send full teams to meetings and include a variety of people on the teams.

Interviewing

One of the best ways a network can evaluate its work is to ask people in the schools about their experiences in implementing the network's premises. Interviewing can help an on-site facilitator understand what is going on in a school, which will help better facilitate a school's work. Interviewing can also help school-based educators reflect on their experiences and how they are feeling about what is happening in their school. This information can be shared with all the member schools so that they benefit from the collective experiences.

During an on-site visit, a facilitator interviews people about the school's implementing the League's three premises: shared governance, an educational focus, and action research. Interviewees are administrators, students, and teachers—holding leadership and nonleadership positions. The facilitator asks them to describe their governance process (conditions of governance), to give examples of the types of issues they have focused on, and to explain how they are determining the effects their shared decisions are having on the school (action research). Since the interview is not an evaluation and because only the school and League staff will see the report, we think people will generally relate accurate information (see Appendix for an on-site visit summary). That information, plus the facilitator's observations, gives both the school and the League staff a snapshot of what the school has accomplished in the past year. Examining the school's on-site visit summaries over four or five years provides a "home movie" of its work, showing movement and growth.

League staff summarize on-site visits and share the findings so that everyone can have a general understanding of where the schools are in implementing the premises. To determine how democratic a school's governance is, we defined a set of conditions that characterizes high, moderate, and low stages of implementation. We decided which educational issues fit in a high impact and which fit in a minimal impact category. We also agreed on the type of actions that characterizes each of the four stages of action research. Over time, we have presented these descriptions to school-based educators, who have agreed that they are acceptable. Developing these stages of implementation and annually summarizing the number of schools in each stage have helped us determine where we (everyone involved in the League) are in our collective work. The summaries provide a sense of direction and accomplishment, and the staff use the information to set the League's annual goals (see Figure 6.1).

Telephone interviews also provide information. Each year, we decide what topic we need to know more about and who in the schools would be in the best position to give us information about that topic. Because these interviews are focused on evaluating the League's effects on schools, we arrange for a person not on the League staff to conduct the interviews, which are recorded and transcribed. League staff analyze the transcripts, with numbers replacing names to protect the interviewees' identities, to learn more about what is happening in schools so that the League can improve its facilitation efforts.

School-Generated Case Studies

School-generated case studies is another way for a network to evaluate itself. Schools study their participation with the network and then write their own case study detailing what they did, how they did it, what the outcomes have been, and the lessons they learned while doing this work. Networks can encourage this process by offering workshops in how to conduct and write a case study, as well as by providing ongoing assistance. Experienced people can mentor others.

Networks can offer guidelines on what should be included in a case study and its approximate length. Offering stipends to those willing to do the work can also

Figure 6.1
Summary of 1994 On-Site Reports from Member Schools of the League of Professional Schools

Year of Membership	SCHOOLS IMPLEMENTING *SHARED GOVERNANCE*					
	Implementation Stage					
	High		*Moderate*		*Low*	
	No.	%	No.	%	No.	%
4th	14	78	3	17	1	5
3rd	11	78	3	22	0	
2nd	7	50	5	36	2	14

Year of Membership	SCHOOLS IMPLEMENTING AN *EDUCATIONAL FOCUS*			
	Implementation Category			
	High Impact		*Minimal Impact*	
	No.	%	No.	%
4th	14	78	4	22
3rd[a]	11	93	1	7
2nd	8	57	6	43

Year of Membership	SCHOOLS IMPLEMENTING *ACTION RESEARCH*							
	Action Research Stage[b]							
	0		*1*		*2*		*3*	
	No.	%	No.	%	No.	%	No.	%
4th[a]	2	12	2	12	5	31	7	45
3rd[a]	0		3	23	2	15	8	62
2nd[a]	4	30	7	54	1	8	1	8

Note: The total number of schools submitting reports is 46: 18 are 4th year; 14 are 3rd year; and 14 are 2nd year.

[a] The number of schools in the year of membership does not equal the number of schools in the categories because not enough information was available to place all the schools in categories.

[b] 0 = no data collected; 1 = data collected; 2 = data analyzed; 3 = actions taken based on data.

encourage the writing. A network can compile and circulate the studies to all member schools.

People from League schools, both individually and as school units, have written 17 case studies over the past three years. The League provides a stipend for writing a case study. We hold one-day, summer workshops conducted by school-based educators who are experienced in writing case studies. Workshop facilitators define the case studies, explain the reasons for writing them, and provide examples. Most of the time is spent working in small groups where individuals considering writing a case study are given the opportunity to try their ideas out on the other group members. Asking questions and making suggestions help each member think through what a case study would look like. By the end of the day, participants have a game plan for how they are going to proceed. In some cases, they have a written outline of what will be included in the study. The writers are encouraged to send drafts to either the League staff or others involved in writing case studies for their feedback. League staff provide copyediting before the study is published.

The League publishes the case studies annually in a monograph that also includes research articles and papers that university associates and League staff have written about League schools. Each League school receives a copy of the monograph.

We have learned from case studies how the League has helped schools address their most important issue—making life better for students. For example, case studies have described how (1) an elementary school created a schoolwide, hands-on science program that dramatically increased students' and teachers' interest in science and led to several students winning science awards and one student attending the U.S. Space Camp; (2) a high school made a change in its daily schedule that better met the needs of all its students; and (3) a middle school implemented a program that increased students' self-esteem and reduced the number of students who were referred to the office for discipline.

Summary

This type of information, which directly links the League's work to school renewal, fuels our growing conviction that our network is benefiting students. We feel strongly that what we are doing, honoring school-based educators' expertise and trusting in the power of democracy, is not an innovation that will soon be replaced by the next "great idea." We wish others interested in this concept well and hope that this book will be of some help. In fact, we have an ulterior motive for encouraging others to form such networks: We envision the creation of a network of networks, where teachers and principals can share their practice across the United States. Such a network could add a vital but missing voice to the current educational dialogue—the voice of school-based educators who, when the time comes to put talk into action, have the last word.

Key Points

- Evaluating a network's efforts is necessary for the network to better serve its members.
- Information gathered while evaluating a network's efforts should be shared with member schools to keep them informed of the network's progress and to help them place their work in context with others doing similar work.
- Collegial on-site visits and written summaries of the visits provide a valuable vehicle for evaluating a network.
- Analyzing schools' actions over time can provide information about patterns and directions that schools are taking in implementing a network's premises.
- Studying school patterns in using the services of a network can help the network identify changes that should be made, as well as help member schools reflect on their use of the services.
- Conducting interviews on how schools are implementing a network's premises and analyzing the responses can provide an understanding of what is happening in schools as a result of their network membership.
- Defining the characteristics for each stage of implementing a network's premises and periodically

summarizing the number of schools that are in each stage can help a network understand where its member schools are in implementing the premises.

• When networks support and encourage schools to write their own case studies detailing what they have done in implementing the network's premises, valuable information is created, both for those facilitating the schools' work and the schools themselves.

Appendix
On-Site Visit Summary

Dear Sunny Day Elementary School,

Thank you for a great day. Your hospitality made me feel at home. What I hope to accomplish with this report is to summarize what was said in the interviews and what I observed during the day. I do not pretend to have an in-depth understanding of your school, but I hope seeing your work through a different lens will stimulate thinking and assist you as you go about the difficult and complex work that you do. My main task as an on-site facilitator was to find out how you feel you are doing in implementing the three premises of the League (shared governance, enhanced education, and action research) and to pick your brains about how you are going about it.

I started my day in the media center as part of the Leadership Team. I was immediately struck by the free flow of thoughts and ideas as the team planned an upcoming meeting for parents. The respect that all ideas were given was obvious. I noticed that nearly everyone participated in the discussion—a perfect example of two heads are better than one. The team was able to take full advantage of everyone's experience and wisdom. I don't know if you take that sort of give-and-take for granted, but I urge you not to. That kind of climate is something to treasure, celebrate, and protect.

Shared Governance

Your shared governance process seemed to be deeply institutionalized. Nearly everyone appears to understand how the process works and is satisfied that it is accomplishing its purpose.

We were especially interested in the changes veteran schools like yours are making. I was able to identify a number of recent adjustments:

1. A teacher is now cochair of the Leadership Team. She is given 40 extra minutes a week to help her with this task. This sharing of responsibility is done in the spirit of spreading out leadership roles in the school and appears to be working.

2. People reported that the Leadership Team is now more focused on student outcomes than it had been.

3. Membership on the Leadership Team is based on grade levels (primary, intermediate, and upper) rather than on specific grade taught.

4. You no longer set new goals each year. They have stayed the same, and the initiatives to meet them are evaluated and adjusted annually.

5. A Conference Committee has been formed to guide the process of deciding who should go to what conferences and meetings. In the past, administrators made this decision.

6. Teachers receive the minutes of Leadership Team meetings instead of seeing them posted in the work room.

7. Working through the Leadership Team, the school, not the central office, decides the school goals.

Several people mentioned that the level of trust between teachers and administrators has greatly improved over the past several years. More teachers see the benefits of taking an active part in the governance of the school. I heard loud and clear the intention to continue to be an inviting school where eventually everyone will be actively involved. To this end, all meetings are open to everyone, and more people are attending. Distributing meeting minutes provides everyone with key information and indicates an intention to have the governance process open to all.

Suggestion: You might want to consider electing representatives to the Leadership Team rather than having the administration appoint them. Such a process is more democratic because it increases teachers' input into the governance process. People may be satisfied with the status quo, however, and not want to change it. You would need to ensure that staff support the change by taking it through the governance process.

Enhanced Education

The focus of your shared governance efforts appears to be squarely on instructional and curricular issues. The three action teams formed around curriculum and instruction; technology; and time and opportunity are the main structures that guide your efforts. Specific initiatives include authentic assessment, performance-based learning, presentation technology (for children), Macintosh and calculator literacy, software for problem solving, inclusion strategies for special education students, and cross-grade groupings. I also heard about ad hoc committees that address the cultural arts, multicultural issues, and media and technology issues. The new Interviewing and Hiring Committee procedures seem well thought out. The committee has great potential for involving teachers in the hiring process.

You have many, many things going on in your school. Is anyone feeling overwhelmed? Are you running the risk of going in too many directions at once? Some schools have reported that they took on too much and had to cut back. I saw no evidence of overcommitment, but I wanted to raise the question.

Action Research

Each Action Team has one person responsible for action research. Your action research initiatives include videotaping interviews of students involved in the new social studies program, conducting surveys on teachers' use of technology in performance-based assessment and students' use of technology in learning and presentations, and collecting School Services Team referral records and discipline referral data. It is too early to report the findings on these efforts. I think that you are in a great position to generate information that will be quite valuable in your decision-making process.

53

You've made several decisions based on data from your action research. For example, data generated last year from a survey on your shared governance process pointed out the need to narrow the focus on what data to gather this year. As action research data are generated, they are made available to all grade level meetings, faculty meetings, *Bear Tracks* [school's newsletter], and in some cases, each teacher.

Your efforts with action research are truly impressive, and your leadership in the League is greatly appreciated. The League will continue to follow your work with an eye to sharing it with other schools.

Teacher and Principal Interviews

How Do You Keep the Ball Rolling?

People mentioned the openness of the decision-making process. Everyone is always invited to be a part of the process and kept well informed on what is going on. Staff appreciate the Hats Off recognition in the school's newsletter. People share what they learn at conferences. A sense of excitement over learning about and incorporating new ideas seems to keep you fired up.

How Has the School Changed Since Joining the League?

People feel freer to express their opinions—diverse thoughts are welcome. Attending League meetings has helped add excitement to the professional lives of many faculty members. You find talking to people from other schools and learning what they are doing helpful. You have incorporated several ideas picked up at League meetings. Some people mentioned that the hardest part of doing this work is building the trust that teachers really will be decision makers. Most people are now convinced that this type of governance is "for real" and are taking part.

What Advice Can You Offer to Others Wanting to Do This Work?

Everyone said that people need to realize that this kind of work takes time and patience. Change can be uncomfortable. Once people see that they will be listened to, the work picks up momentum.

Student Interviews

When I asked how they would describe their school, students said it was a friendly place: Most students are friendly, and most teachers are nice. They explained that nice teachers don't yell; they look into situations before assigning blame; and they make things exciting (gave examples of hands-on types of activities).

When I asked how decisions were made in classrooms, students said that teachers are the main decision makers. They mentioned that some teachers have class votes on things like parties, student council representatives, and star students. They pointed out that the student council will decide the school theme after receiving input from other students, and they were enthusiastic about this opportunity.

When I asked how decisions were made about what goes on in the school, they mentioned the principal and assistant principals. They said that teachers have a lot of meetings where they talk about "things," and that the principals would probably not make a decision without talking to teachers first.

Their suggestions for ways to make the school even better were (1) have skating night more often, (2) have more books, (3) make school "funner," and (4) work more with partners (one student said it was good or bad, depending on whether your partner did his or her share of the work).

Thank you for an enlightening day. Getting into schools and seeing all the wonderful things that are going on is always an enriching experience. Please don't hesitate to contact us if we can be of help. The League will continue to call on you for your expertise.

Sincerely,
John Smith
(Teacher, Green Hill Elementary School)

References and Resources

Allen, L., and C.D. Glickman. (1992). "School Improvement: The Elusive Faces of Shared Governance." *NASSP Bulletin* 76, 542: 80-87.

Firestone, W.A., and B.D. Bader. (1992). *Redesigning Teaching: Professionalism or Bureaucracy.* Albany: State University of New York Press.

Glickman, C.D. (1990). "Pushing School Reform to a New Edge: The Seven Ironies of Empowerment." *Phi Delta Kappan* 72, 1: 68-75.

Glickman, C.D. (1991). "Pretending Not to Know What We Know." *Educational Leadership* 48, 8: 4-10.

Glickman, C.D. (1992). "The Essence of School Renewal: The Prose Has Begun." *Educational Leadership* 50, 1: 24-27.

Glickman, C.D. (1993). *Renewing America's Schools: A Guide for School-Based Action.* San Francisco: Jossey-Bass.

Glickman, C.D. (n.d.). *Shared Governance at Oglethorpe County High School.* Athens: Program for School Improvement, University of Georgia.

Glickman, C.D. (presenter). (1994). *Site-Based Governance* (videotape). Vol. 3, no. 5. Sandy, Utah: The Video Journal of Education.

Glickman, C.D., L.R. Allen, and B.F. Lunsford. (1994). "Voices of Principals from Democratically Transformed Schools." In *Reshaping the Principalship: Insights from Transformational Reform Efforts,* edited by J. Murphy and K.S. Louis. Thousand Oaks, Calif.: Corwin Press.

Glickman, C.D., L.R. Allen, and B.F. Lunsford. (In Press). "Facilitation of School Renewal: Lessons from the League." *Journal of Staff Development.*

Hanson, L., L. Allen, and C. Glickman, eds. (1991–1993). 3 vols. *Lessons from the Field: Improving Schools Through Shared Governance and Action Research.* Athens: Program for School Improvement, University of Georgia.

In-Sites. Biannual newsletter of the League of Professional Schools. Athens: Program for School Improvement, University of Georgia.

Lieberman, A., and M. McLaughlin. (1992). "Networks for Educational Change: Powerful and Problematic." *Phi Delta Kappan* 73, 9: 673-677.

Short, P.M., and J.T. Greer. (1993). "Restructuring Schools Through Empowerment." In *Restructuring Schooling: Learning from Ongoing Efforts,* edited by J. Murphy and P. Hallinger. Newbury Park, Calif.: Corwin Press.

Smylie, M.A. (1994). "Redesigning Teachers' Work: Connections to the Classroom." In *Review of Research in Education*, edited by L. Darling-Hammond. Washington, D.C.: American Educational Research Association.